Look LEGO City

J K Pattinson

The Town

Look at the town.

Can you see the bin?
Can you see the man?

The Farm

Look at the farm.

Can you see the dog?
Can you see the pigs?

The Airport

Look at the airport.

Can you see the man?
Can you see the bags?

Picture Index

 airport 6–7

 farm 4–5

 town 2–3